The Day Before

Also by Dick Allen

Ode to the Cold War: Poems New and Selected (1997)
Flight and Pursuit (1987)
Overnight in the Guest House of the Mystic (1984)
Regions with No Proper Names (1975)
Anon and Various Time Machine Poems (1971)

The Day Before

NEW POEMS ~~Dick Allen~~

Dick Allen

To Shesr,

These poems of fields and computers, some short, some long, some ...

With all best wishes for your own poetry,

Dick

Sarabande S Books

LOUISVILLE, KENTUCKY

Hill-Stead, Oct, 2004

No part of this book may be reproduced without written permission of the publisher. Please direct inquiries to:

> Managing Editor
> Sarabande Books, Inc.
> 2234 Dundee Road, Suite 200
> Louisville, KY 40205

Library of Congress Cataloging-in-Publication Data

Allen, Dick, 1939–
    The day before : new poems / by Dick Allen.— 1st ed.
    p. cm.
  ISBN 1-889330-75-2 (hardcover : alk. paper) — ISBN 1-889330-76-0 (pbk. : alk. paper) I. Title.
PS3551.L3922 D39 2003
811'.54—dc21   2002007225

Cover image: *Spring Turning*, by Grant Wood. Oil masonite panel, 1936.
© Estate of Grant Wood/Licensed by VAGA, New York, NY.

Cover and text design by Charles Casey Martin.

Manufactured in the United States of America.
This book is printed on acid-free paper.

Sarabande Books is a nonprofit literary organization.

 This project is supported in part by an award from the National Endowment for the Arts, and by the Kentucky Arts Council, a state agency of the Education, Arts, and Humanities Cabinet.

FIRST EDITION

in the memory of Lucy Allen Heath

TABLE OF CONTENTS

THREE

ACKNOWLEDGMENTS

Grateful acknowledgement is given to the editors and publishers of the following, in which some of these poems first appeared, a few in slightly different versions:

American Arts Quarterly, "And Leave My Human Feelings...,"
  "Rime Forest"
The Antioch Review, "[Say We Have to Name the World Again]"
Atlanta Review, "In Wyeth Country," "Jubilate"
The Atlantic Monthly, "Memo from the Desk of Wallace Stevens,"
  Part II of "The Litany of Disparagement"
The Bible of Hell (Pendragonian Publications, 2000), "The Back
  of God"
Boulevard, "Lost Friends"
The Café Review, "The Selfishness of the Poetry Reader"
The Cortland Review, "Poem for My Sixtieth Birthday"
Crab Orchard Review, "On Roark's Farm," "Sunday"
Family Reunion: Poems by Parents of Grown Children (Chicory
  Blue Press, 2003), "The Children"
The Gettysburg Review, "The Father Suite," "Some Man I Knew"
Hampden-Sydney Poetry Review, "Urban Pastoral"
The Hudson Review, "The Cove," "Letter to Ye Feng, His Student
  Now in Iowa," "Poem for Li in Her White Bridal Dress"

Image: A Journal of the Arts and Religion, "The Devotion of
   Thomas Merton"

*Intelligence There with Passion: A Festschrift in Honor of Frederick
   Morgan's Fiftieth Anniversary at* The Hudson Review (Aralia
   Press, 1998), "Intuition"

Margie, "A Shadowy Government Agency"

Mid-American Review, "The Simile"

The New Criterion, "The Familiar," "Ferns," "Homefront"

The New Republic, "Then"

North American Review, "Letter to One Who May Be Dead
   or Not"

The Ontario Review, "Triptych," "This Far"

*Photographers, Writers, and the American Scene: Visions of
   Passage* (Arena Editons, 2002), "The Day Before Yesterday,"
   "Quiet, Quiet Now"

Pivot, "Animus," "The Green Children"

Ploughshares, "Cassandra in Connecticut"

Poetry, "The American Zen Master," "Being Taught," "God Gives
   to Every Bird . . . ," "Man of the Cloth," "Texas Prison Town,"
   "Zen Living"

Poetry Review (England), "Although the Temporal is Beautiful"

Quarterly West, "If You Get There Before I Do," "Vehicle"

Rosebud, "April"

Salmagundi, "After Reading Tichborne's Elegy"

Smartish Pace, "After a Proverb by William Blake," "Bishop Eyes"

The Yale Review, "A Boy Called Vanish"

"The Cove" was reprinted in *The Best American Poetry: 1998.*

"The Selfishness of the Poetry Reader" was reprinted in *The Best American Poetry: 1999.*

"The American Zen Master," "Simile," "God Gives to Every Bird . . . ," and "Vehicle" were reprinted on *Poetry Daily.*

"And Leave My Human Feelings..."

The world, as we know it, will cease to exist,
Schrödinger's cat will live / Schrödinger's cat will die.
The towers on the rock will turn to mist.

An open palm is hidden by a fist,
And what screamed here is not what happened by.
The world, as we know it, will cease to exist.

Amethyst to coal, and coal to amethyst.
That dragon in the field's no dragonfly.
The towers on the rock will turn to mist.

The heart of each life's story is its sudden twist.
Even the dullest child can grow a weather eye.
The world, as we know it, will cease to exist.

When thwarted lover turns to terrorist,
Perverting God to set himself On High,
The towers on the rock will turn to mist.

Backlist, checklist, snake hiss, deathlist.
I saw a huge 11 fall down from the sky.
The world, as we know it, will cease to exist.
The towers on the rock will turn to mist.

And these ideas, which constitute reality, are names, as nominalism showed. Not that they may not be more than names, but that they are nothing less than names. Language is that which gives us reality, and not as a mere vehicle of reality, but as its true flesh.... And thus logic operates upon aesthetics, the concept upon the expression, upon the word....

Language and Philosophers
Miguel De Unamuno Y Jungo

ONE

A Boy Called Vanish

He was about drainpipes, spyglasses, red Pegasus
on a Mobil sign,
and knew, as other boys didn't, he was vanishing
like the first innings of a baseball game,
but couldn't stop it. He was about
how you count to ten and look around
for nobody there. While everyone slept,
he wound his wristwatch backward and uncombed his hair,
whispering *"Shazam! Shazam!"* He wore
brown corduroy pants; he lost
footprints in the snow across the fields
to black and white birches. To see him,
you had to be as careful as a lock and key
or the soul of forgiveness. Everyone else
saw only that he wasn't them and turned their heads
into their sorrows. He collected
moods of small houses, ripples on the lake,
and when he bicycled the evening roads,
old Fords up on blocks and backyard girls
clinging to their mothers' hands. He was
watching himself vanish into me
and hated but accepted how I gave him books
to speed him on his way,
and my dog Buck to guard him from all harm.

Homefront

Sunflowers grew so tall in the Coshburns' garden,
ten, twelve feet before a night windstorm
flattened them, decapitating some
(whose heads we found floating in the road,
and dangling from the wire mesh of a rabbit warren),
they frightened us . . . as if they were children who become
adults too soon, the darkness at their roots
sensed by other children—as I remember
sensing the coming beauty of Nancy Parker,
the death of Billy Meade. The sunflowers
grew uglier and uglier, a dozen higher ones
with faces descending at us from between
invisible shoulders, faces grotesquely swaying
on horrible stalks. And yet the Coshburns
seemed not to notice. Blithely, they beckoned us
closer and closer. Look up and see the sun,
they said. Don't you wish that you and you
could grow so tall. The night they fell,
moths bumped our windowscreens, the radio
went static, then dead. My mother screamed
at her clothesline. From the upstairs porch
of our summer cottage, lightning serifs melting
all over the sky, I watched the Coshburns' garden
as the sunflowers, one by one, went down,
splayed like compass points; and I was glad
the forces beyond us were protecting us

even in the small towns of upstate New York,
in 1945, in that hot war-torn July.

Triptych

The lake beyond the two boys playing basketball
    does not shimmer. It's simply a gray wash
below a few unfocused hills
    so low and commonplace no one's yet named them,
and the house in the foreground, with the old
    Dodge up on blocks beside it isn't worth
even a glance. Why enter it? Inside,
    the mirrors will be dusty, the furniture a few
dark pieces scattered on some thin gray rugs,
    nothing that would make you climb the stairs
to the bedroom in back, its single window
    facing the lake, beneath it an old half-rotted
picnic table salvaged from a dump, the circular
    clothesline in a square of ragged bushes....
Yet this isn't poverty. The boys are fed
    sufficiently, and loved. The roads
you can't see joining other roads
    are passable, the cities at their ends—
thick airstrips leading off to Vietnam,
    Nicaragua hot beneath the moon—
no dream. All reaches and is reached from here,
    even on this day my father stands outside
and lifts his Kodak, takes his undistinguished
    photograph of house and car and lake and bare

tree branches cluttering, haphazardly, the white
    November sky. And like an afterthought
or because they happened to be there,
    too small and distant to be waved away,
two boys.

      II

        What were his thoughts? What were
my mother's thoughts outside her magazine
    ambitions for her sons? *Gray Saturdays.*
The radiator cat. Schoolboy friends
    killed at Normandy. The never-ending wish
and want! When the lake froze over
    we'd walk a mile across it toward the dark
and gutted icehouse. "Listen!" my father would shout
    into a broken window. *Listen, listen . . . listen*
his voice would echo. Then retracing
    our snowcrust path, we made our way out on
the lake again, ice booming, and the mist
    of slight wind-scattered snow so gossamer
we'd lift our mittened hands to part it constantly.
    White eyebrows and hot cocoa and the game of Clue
my mother always won. All reaches. All is reached
    from here. Chernobyl. The fattened goosenecked cloud
of the Challenger. Nixon waving. Dallas.
    Press of fingers on computer buttons.
The Chinese horns and hellgates of Korea.

Hiroshima. Dresden. "The Eyes and Ears of the World."
The Holocaust.... You touch my arm
    to bring me out of it. Dulled, dazed,
approaching sixty with my hands still balancing
    a basketball, knees bent, my eyes
sighting to the hole in space above the rim,
    I fire. The world arcs up. My father fires....

                    III

        Listen, listen ... listen
his voice would echo. But for what? For why?
    Not even half a century has passed since I
first heard him shouting in those charred-wood rafters
    and the booming of the ice, the fleck, fleck
of dry snow scraped by boots—and one day for an hour
    with my Gilbert microscope upon the picnic table,
I tested the hypothesis of no
    snowflake shaped the same—and in that world
of crystal symmetry, found such elegance
    and mystery I thought I might reach God
through search, not prayer. Mistake. How blurred
    was my belief.... In the photograph
two edges and one chimney of the cottages
    whose lots touched ours; a section of the fence
around the village's cracked tennis court;
    a streetlamp that will soon come on,
the boys will stand beneath. They'll toss

                    8

the basketball, bounce-pass it, dribble it
until their hands are raw. No one will take
    their picture at this hour—soon not even they
remember what they say: passing the ball, brilliantly
    catching it behind their backs and whipping it
away, away. Up to the moon. Up to the stars,
    away, away.... When they're gone
perhaps it rains or snows. Ice freezes
    on every twig and branch, catching the streetlamp's glow
in such a way a web of light is spun
    around it until dawn. No color in the frame.
November day, then night.... Two boys playing ball.

The Father Suite

I. Steady as She Goes

"Steady as she goes," my father would yell,
Steering the boat we rented that only summer
He had any money,
Between the buoys and the other, larger

Boats all around us. His bald head covered
With a skipper's cap, its emblem
A small gold anchor on a field of black,
He'd stand at the helm

Laughing for dear life. "Steady as she goes,
Steady as she goes." The ocean
He sailed us out on, I remember to this day,
Was calm as a silver coin

Near the shore, but roughened out deeper,
Waves melting and reforming lee and starboard,
Bow and aft. "Beautiful, beautiful, beautiful,"
He'd say. Then toward

Noon he'd becalm us. From an icy chest,
Red pop and sandwiches, their crusts
Meant to be torn off
And thrown to any gulls at rest

On the sea's path.... The next year,
Back in poverty's pit, a tenement
Of boarded windows, light bulbs hung from cords,
Where my mother scrubbed dirt from dirt and found more dirt,

He'd sit backward on his kitchen chair
And staring out at a clothesline fat with clothes,
Pretend, with us, they were sails
Filled with wind blows

As the blue sheets billowed and the thin skirts spun
Around on their hangers. "Steady as she goes," he'd whisper,
"Steady as she goes"—but not sorry for himself.
Don't think that, ever. I remember

When everything ached in him—you could hear it
In his voice and feel it in his arms
Trying to hug us goodnight, but clutching
Instead—he'd still not damn

The world, nor himself, nor us....
Why is life
So cruel? Surely it has a heart, but why's that heart
So punctured and ruptured? If

The breaks had gone right...but they didn't. If
He hadn't had children.... Out on that boat
When evening started to come and the lighthouse blinked
From the shore, like a tiny star in a net

11

Of low-lying clouds, he'd grow so silent
Looking down at us, feet spread to keep his balance,
It was as if his mind was lost, he'd never
Get us back home. But then he'd wince

Abruptly, shake his head from side to side
And find his voice again.... I've caught myself
Doing the same thing lately. It's
Just that there's so much grief

About, and to deal with—beauty and grief. I can't
Reconcile them well.... Slowly, not more than a quarter-inch
Over stalling speed, he'd steer us in,
Calling to other skippers, his nautical speech

Too proud to be rusty. "Steady as she goes," he'd sing
To the harbor and gas pumps and piers
We passed. To the wind-bent trees
In the coves, the houses and flashy cars

On the last viaduct we barely floated under
Before we docked. "Steady as she goes,"
He'd say one more time, after we'd tied
The ropes taut, and carefully hosed

Down the decks. Then, grandly sweeping his cap
As he bowed like an English admiral courting a lady,

He'd have our mother walk before him up the wooden ramp
To the parking lot. Gladly, he'd follow.... Gladly,

And I think knowingly, he burned his money up
That summer. "Good day, really good day,"
I can still hear him saying as he drove
Our ripped-seat Studebaker with its gray

Half-working dashboard
Into the city, holding an even thirty-six
Miles-per-hour because of, or despite
The eternally heavy traffic

Veering around us.... Beauty and grief, or maybe you
Can find some other words. Was it a foolish pose
Or blend of risk and caring? Does it matter which?
He kept our life here steady, steady as she goes.

II. Heart Condition

"You would take their side!" my mother screamed
    at my father
when the ambulance he'd finally summoned came,
    and she kicked and bit as they took her

from Aspinwall Drive,
    where she'd been trying to compel her heart back,

keep it alive
    on a diet of carrot sticks

and her famous will power. Tied down, sedated,
    eight hours later, she died.
Her heart literally burst. He'd waited
    and he'd cried

in her hospital room, begging to her, but she never
    spoke to him again,
went out of this world blaming others,
    scorning *that man*

who as she'd bloated then terribly thinned gave up
    his own life to help her plan
how she'd recover—she, a typical Bishop;
    and he, a typical Allen.

III. Breath

"He walked out on the prairie and he shot himself,"
    his wife said.
"Brains all over. Blood.
I think now I'll travel.... "

"Another life," writes my father, "gone with the wind,
    to cite Margaret Mitchell.

14

I always liked that title.
Your mother read that book from start to end

again and again." He's moved up to Idaho—
after her death—starting over,
living close to my brother.
This summer in the mountains he found heavy snow

blocking the road and backed his Jeep a mile
before he could turn.
He's given up trying to learn
to follow her principles

of good diet, proper dress—his hearing aid
often turned off.
He's been "a good boy" long enough,
he says, and too often afraid.

His emphysemic neighbor in the next-door condominium
told him he hadn't slept
for three nights running, then kept
his promise to himself to end the pain,

left his nose-tubes and his oxygen at home,
walked out on the prairie
that morning, very early.
"The day," my father says, "was a very pretty one."

IV. Those Who Are Surpassed

"Their eyes are always bigger than their stomachs,"
my father said,
"that's how you can tell them: big eyes,
little thin stomachs.

"At the table of life
they always heap too much and never finish."
Not him.
His plate was always cleared, he always kept

just a little room left over for dessert: Bavarian
creme pies,
deep dark chocolate cakes,
syrup floating up the edges of bread puddings,

and smacked his lips and seemed content, while those
around him groaned
and nibbled with embarrassment the rich
concoctions he'd planned for

with calculating visions and a loosened belt. "You see,
the secret's in the appetite," he said, "to know
what's possible
and what's impractical. One taste at a time,"

he said, "one delicious bite and savor it, and then
the next,"

who lived to ninety, gained tremendous girth
and died without a speck

of usual regret—his several books, his articles, his meals
completed in a lonely condominium in Idaho,
the dishes washed,
and he asleep within his great armchair.

Bishop Eyes

"Yes, he's ours, he has them," I remember
Grandmother Sadie (on my mother's side)
exclaim while leaning over our new son,
"the Bishop eyes."

My wife—three-quarters Slavic, great-great-great
granddaughter of a Russian countess—sighed
and rolled her own. In her family line
the Tartars and the Mongols always vied

in each new child—first one
emerging, then the other, in haphazard leaps
down through the genes. "You see,
the slant, the lovely almond shape,"

Grandmother Sadie said. "The girls
will all be after him." Somewhere,
some deep dark somewhere in our family tree,
a concubine from Canton or perhaps

a disgraced Peking lady from an outcast clan
that for a decade once ruled dynasties,
must have entered us, as if—truly—yes
her eyes became "the Bishop eyes"—and I've

seen them also in my uncles and my cousins' sons
(the gene is male and dominant and skips
generations as it runs). So I've come
also to believe

the Bishop eyes will last—no matter what
attacks them from the West.
The woman carried in them won't stay hidden
or suppressed

but looking up into our Occidental skies
shall find bronze doors of temples in the clouds,
brushstrokes and the missionary tracts,
then be cast down

and out . . . through my son . . . and in turn
his male grandchild, *ad infinitum*,
at their puzzled mothers holding them,
bemused and graced by mysteries they'd borne . . .

and Grandmother Sadie cooed, and wiggling her
arthritic fingers said again,
"Bishop eyes. Blue almonds. All the same,
those Bishop eyes."

"God Gives to Every Bird Its Proper Food but They Must All Fly for It"

My aunt, drowning in birdcalls, telephones
to say a wren has built its nest within
the little thoughts of her TV. A cardinal
is flying backward through her porcelain

and she can't stand it. Sparrows
have found the seeds among her early days;
a plover's lit upon her love of Charlotte Brontë,
her kitchen's filled with hopping chickadees,

what should she do? In her weakened state,
she cannot shoo them from their scurrying
across her long-held views and windowsills,
and one is pulling at her last heartstring

as if it's just some worm come out in the rain,
forced up from the soil in search of warmth.
A hawk is diving toward her Wyeth plate,
two grackles bite a prejudice to death

and even as she speaks, a mockingbird
is making toward her bed. My aunt,
who played the violin for Bernstein once,
adored his eyebrows and his stiff starched pants,

rode in rumble seats, and thought she saw
Picasso in a brothel sipping chocolate shakes,
has no will left, she says. The mourning doves
have claimed her closets for their own. Pine Siskins take

liberties, such liberties. A thousand miles away,
I hold the hambone into which she weeps,
and hear, behind her voice, the purple finch,
the evening grosbeak, and the rapt bluejays.

After Reading Tichborne's Elegy

The world shrinks to a face within a face,
The kind you sometimes see on the evening news
Bearded with microphones, its outer outline
Almost the same as yours, but behind it
Eyes that have seen the death of children, villages
Rubbled in hours, a mouth too slack to scream,
The face of our time. You look away. After all,
Pain is a commonplace and you have felt it
Often enough in your life—if not at this
Blanked-out intensity, still you have watched
Presidents go down on the sidewalks, ambulances
Traveling dark roads, and heard in the night wind
Wings beating, and shrieking of something caught
Too small to matter. Often, your living room
Seems lighted by pitch-pine torches, the interior
Of an Egyptian burial chamber, all the things you love
At hand: perfumes, paintings, flasks of wine,
Tablets of chants and prayers. Such richness would
Appall the ancient kings.... You rise from your couch,
Seeing the face again. In the golden light
It floats and weeps. If you could speak to it
You might ask forgiveness, but it does not see you
Or your awkwardness. Once, when you were walking
A low road through the Scottish moors, you found
Concealed by heather, a face with a child's puffed cheeks
Carved on a wayside stone, and an inscription

Too blurred to read except for the words *Jesu*

And *Merci*. The larks cried overhead; you kept

So still you could almost make out human speech

Among them. And then a storm like a clothed fist

Struck at you, you hurried on toward the village

Through gusts of warm rain.... You think of strangers,

Thousands of them, passing you in a mall,

Cirrus clouds laid low, each one that passes,

A tiny mystery: you are walking

Constantly through their slowly moving edges

As they are through yours. What is required,

Or if not required, allowed? And if you have

The will to change the world, yet lack the power,

Are you accomplished in the eyes of God?

In the cedars of Lebanon, the face appears;

And it is looking from a second-story window

Over the Harlem River; and it is in a snowstorm

Beating on Afghanistan. So is it too

On the movie screen of a bird-beaked Concorde above

The Pacific, reflects from silvered glasses

Worn on the Riviera. Always, it stares through you

And you grow dizzy with too much reproach and grasp

The fireplace mantel for balance while the vase

Of butterfly weed, daisies, clover, black-eyed Susans

Trembles before you. To take all this in!

And you think of Tichborne writing in his tower,

Of his darkened hourglass, his unspun thread,

The dawn come like a boat upon the Thames.

World images replace the limited

Visions of your country torn halfway apart
As you turn the cable channels, finding one
Ashen and silent. You stare into its gray
Face, for in the static say astronomers
Are signals from the time the universe
Began. On this dark planet, kneeling here,
You tune the voices other beings may
Have traveled on, until the algebraic storm
Crests upon you and you lift your head
Once more from all things asking you to live
For those who suffer, all who speak no longer
Of terror, wonder, and you see upon the wall
Your print of Wood's *Stone City* where a man
Rides a huge white dray beside a windmill
Still as everything the artist froze to stone:
Stone bridge, stone river, and great fields of stone
That will not break though you must strike at them.
Strike hard, strike fast, but strike most out of love.
Cling to this day until its flanks are stone.

The Children

Not you, but what they made of you
is what they've taken
to shape their lives.

Not you, but some monster
who walked across a field in a golden sweater
while they trailed behind.

Not you, but a pair of eyes,
a wet flash of anger,
or some approving smile for some small thing they did.

You teasing or laughing,
skipping stones across some placid river,
back there in their minds.

Not you, but something in some other world
of their own making,
looking down on them—or praising

what they can't praise themselves.
You frozen in time,
the you that is not you forever theirs.

Two

Everyday examples are legion. Just take the local main street. Is there a fabric shop or not? Many people have lived near a specialist outlet for years and never known it was there—until the day they needed just such a store and either are directed to it or spot it themselves. Afterward they cannot imagine how they managed to wander along that street so many times in ignorance of the shop's existence.

> *The User Illusion: Cutting Consciousness Down to Size*
> Tør Norretranders

Zen Living

Birdsongs that sound like the steady determined tapping
of a shoemaker's hammer,
or of a sculptor making tiny ball-peen dents in a silver plate,
wake me this morning. *Is it possible*
the world itself can be happy? The calico cat
stretches her long body out across the top of my computer monitor,
yawning, its little primitive head a cave of possibility.
And I'm ready again
to try and see accidents, the over and over patterns
of double-slit experiments a billionfold
repeated before me. If I had great patience,
I could try to count the poplar, birch, and oak
leaves in their shifting welter outside my bedroom window
or the almost infinitesimal trails of thought that flash and flash
everywhere, as if decaying particles inside a bubble chamber,
windshield raindrops, lake ripples. However,
instead I go to fry some bacon, crack two eggs
into the cast-iron skillet that's even older than this house,
and on the calendar (each month another oriental fan
where the climbing solitary is dwarfed ... or on dark blue oceans
minuscular fishing boats bob beneath gigantic waves)
X out the days, including those I've forgotten.

Intuition

It's not in your face. It says in quiet tones,
"I will help you."
It drives an ordinary car on ordinary roads
into the flames

no one else will see for many years. It listens
like a young man in love,
so far down inside a happiness
it moves pebbles and stones.

It wears its sleeves turned up above the elbows,
blinks in spotlights, cuts its way
through tripwires and English hedges,
delivers messages that glow

faintly as a low-turned halogen
lamp in the corner of a poet's bedroom. It
is deceptive
but without anxiety. It has

surveyed what it needs to know of farms and stars
and dismissed the rest. *"I will help you,"*
it whispers in doorways,
"I will help you, I will lift you up."

In Wyeth Country

In Wyeth country, where the Brandywine
Flows beneath rusted iron bridges, and in October
Each hill has a barn with white light shining through it,

And chaff swirls on the floor,
There is such calm
Waiting with ordinary faces by the windows,

It is almost unrendable. *Who commanded us*
To spend our lives in such slow work, to age
Long before we were ready,

To sit by these windows, hands in lap, and stare
At skies so blank of detail they could belong
To any country? In Wyeth country,

The house leans, the church is a shell,
Farmroads tilt into the fields and disappear
Like thoughts we follow to a ridge and lose

In other thoughts. *Brick. Stone. Wood.* And here
A plow in a furrow, a stump no chains could budge,
Glass broken from a smoky shaving mirror.

Rime Forest

That beauty near-death voyagers describe,
    returned to their bodies with heart thumps,
or try to describe before they realize words
    are to the eternal as the dark is to a lamp,

might be close to this, as if we've entered
    a mile long hologram of spiral nebulae
or the neuro-networks of a frozen brain,
    everything glazed and glistening, clarified

in a silence of hanging wind chimes, even the smallest
    twig an icy capillary, every millet blade
diamond-spined. Walk for a moment
    over the snow crust and the sound is stiff brocade,

the feeling slight gliding. Every reflection
    seems a further facet of a farther star,
and at the nexus of white galaxies,
    synaptic leapings in the sycamore,

ski trails down a broken milkweed pod,
    a crystal river through the interstice
of two larch boughs. Every branch and needle
    backlit by each other, Victorian lace,

chandelier pine cones, the last jet vapor trails
   crisscrossed in a fallen maple leaf.
Breathe slowly, look long. In only hours
   bedraggled life will reassert itself

and shaking melted colors from the sun,
   tend onwards as dawn. In a day or less,
mud and rocks and damaged undergrowth,
   the basal rosettes of the winter cress.

Ferns

Almost invisible, but once you look for them
nearly everywhere
like moss in crevices and drifting thoughts,

ferns are what it must mean
to love without yearning. Protectors
of everything small that needs to disappear,

deer mice and tossed trash, bad brushstrokes in a painting,
theirs is the softest name, the softest touch.
They are social workers

as social workers should be—so full of calm
even those who don't trust them
come into their care. Fiddleheads or not,

the rumor that once a year, on Midsummer's Eve,
ferns blossom with tiny blue flowers
and if a pinch of fern seed falls upon your shoes

you will be less apparent—this rumor
is baseless: ferns have tiny spores
that travel in dew and raindrops,

no more magical

than Henri Rousseau composing *The Peaceable Kingdom,*

or adder's tongues, cinnamon, wall rue.

In the world's secret corners,

men wish to vanish, but ferns are what look on,

trembling, holding all light green places.

Strip Malls

Even new, out on some leaving-the-city road
among the auto dealerships, small manufacturers,
and tool and die shops,
they always seem in danger of going under:
the tiny laundromat with no one in it,
Tony's Pizza closed, a few blue-haired ladies
in front of the three-aisle Rexall's;
the last gasp of the famous jewelry store
tarred and feathered, driven from downtown;
the ubiquitous bank with its tellers who have no last names
you've chatted up for years and suddenly they vanish,
swept away in a merger.
             Even when their parking lots are almost full
and teenagers lean about the Coke machines,
looking stupid as boiled carrots, as cool as fresh spit,
these strip malls, remember,
have, as Matthew Arnold said about the world,
"... *neither joy, nor love, nor light,*
nor certitude, nor help from pain." They were
conceived for profit, they'll go down for profit,
so ugly, so utilitarian, they'll leave
only in the mind the smudge of burning rubber,
a packet of Equal and a few McDonald's wrappers,
no torso of Apollo, no panther in a cage,
nothing about them inspired,
             no one who entered them changed.

Quiet, Quiet Now

As in crossing over the Bourne Bridge
　　onto the Cape's curled lobster claw;
as in walking through a redwood forest,
　　hands brushing the ferns;
as in the way mist clears from Crater Lake,
　　leaving that hallowed blue of snow shadows;
as in the shade of regimental monuments
　　off by themselves in Antietam's evening fields;
as in the middle of Kansas
　　where all there seems to be is wheat and sky;
as in a glass-bottomed boat
　　backing and idling over a coral reef;
as in the trapezoid buttes of Montana,
as in the holy woods of upper Maine,
as in the Storm King Mountain sculptures of David Smith,
as in the ghost towns of Idaho,
as in the Frank Lloyd Wright house where a black piano
　　still hangs suspended over narrow stairs;
as in the light that falls into a Hopper painting,
　　as on a porch in lower Michigan;
as how a memory of calm
　　is like a tall and graceful woman in a summer gown
　　standing on the porch, holding the screen door open....

The Simile

What it is like
is what it never is: a thing apart,
neither the joined nor what the joined joins to,
invisible love that nonetheless exists,
the almost but the never quite,
a yoking that, when seen, forever vanishes
into opposites. It's like
a faulty, although useful, rubber band
stretched between a finger and a thumb,
contains its own disclaimer and creates
its own sort of tension. It becomes
one and another and a third,
like the Christian Trinity or Buddha's hand
holding a pebble that is like the world
and once it is imagined it joins us
in ways no dogmatist could understand,
being caught behind fences, doomed
to the lie of the equal or not,
the lie of the either/or,
the metaphor
that's like a river crossing where a bridge has been blown down,
assimilation, war.

The Green Children

> In the end I was so overwhelmed by the weight of so many
> competent witnesses, that I have been compelled to believe
> and wonder over a matter that I was unable to comprehend
> or unravel by the powers of my intellect.
>
> William of Newburg
> *Historia Rerum Anglicarum*

They gave us beans to eat. Before, we ate nothing,

As we were unacquainted with the bread and water.

Of how we came here, I have little feeling.

There was the sound of bells and there were caverns

Through which we wandered long. The reapers found us

Near the wolfpits, and my brother struggled

Harder than I. He died a few weeks hence, his skin

Changing, but still green. Of better appetite,

I lived, I lost my color, and I later married

A man of Lynn, to whom I bore white babes.

I was lily-of-the-valley leaves, my hair

Like green moss by the brookside, and my clothes

Shimmered as the forest mist at twilight

So they burned them, thinking them bewitched. I chose

To speak but little of my father's house

But truth was, I remembered much. They claimed

We were of Merlin's Land, where no sun rises, falls,

Yet a brightness reigns. Child, did you cross

That river cast between us, asked a parish priest.

I did not, answered I, nor doubt the Holy Ghost.

Near Coggeshall, my brother's tiny grave. The grass
Grows thicker, taller there. Would that he lived
To relearn merriment. Sometimes I bring
My babes to play their foolish hide and seek
Among these tongues of stone, then hear the bells
Ring out upon the glebe. I do not understand
Why I was saved, what purpose brought me hence,
Nor do I care. I trust the Lord. I am content.
Let others hear our story and be mystified.
Green grow the rushes and the land is green.

The American Zen Master

Zen also is to be found, he tried to instruct us,

in a car dealer's showroom, and in shoelaces.... Also, in America,

you don't sit at the feet of the Zen Master

but you have coffee with him, preferably at Starbucks,

next to one of those outsized suburban malls where everyone
    looks half dressed,

half dazed and half dead. *"The secret of Zen,"* the Master said,

"may come halfway through a Yankee Candle store

when you realize you can smell nothing,

or from reading Hallmark Cards backwards,

or choosing nothing from an overstuffed refrigerator. But it isn't
    a secret."

                    As for our questions,

instead of smiting us around the shoulders with a bamboo cane,

he'd hand us little writing-intensive packets of Equal and
    Sweet 'N Low,

then lean back, smiling like a sushi plate. Sometimes, he'd babble:

"Tums, drive-up windows, ATM machines.

Checkout line scanners, 1000 Megahertz,

the industrial landscapes so remarkable." Often

we'd catch him staring at the intricate face

of a digital wristwatch, or contemplating

a simple button-down shirt on a white shelf in a Wal-Mart.

All things. *"Throw your computers into the eyes of children,"*

he loved to tell us. *"Work for the Federal administration,*

if that's what you must.

Wear last year's fashions, re-endure the 80s.

Take the last train to Clarksville.

If you meet the Buddha on the road, kill her." We'd come to Zen

because everything else seemed about the mystery, not of it,

and all we could think about for days was money,

Internet cable, huge pasta dishes. Our pain is real, we said.

The only words we have to describe our lives

are "Please wake us!" Our Zen Master

was patient. Our Zen Master assigned us these exercises: "Tie
   your shoes.

Open doors. Close them. Gaze

into the heart of a microwave. Fold a piece of paper eight times
   into halves.

Present yourself with the present." Still, we puzzled.

Riding Chevrolets into the dark, we'd turn around to find

only a series of accidents strewn behind us,

our dead mothers, our dead fathers, our dead friends.

And when he'd say *"Focus on what's in store windows,"* we could
   see the Obvious

and where the Obvious came from, and beyond the Obvious,

but the Obvious eluded us. I thought it was William James,

our love of Marilyn Monroe. He said it was the Suburu of
   Wiltshire Boulevard

and to give it more time. He didn't care. We shouldn't care.

No one should care. One evening,

he mentioned the greatest work is not to work at all.

So difficult. *So difficult to do nothing*

but gaze at the Momentum. The small boats upon the Momentum.

   We didn't get it.

We'd spread our wings and all they'd brushed was air.

He laughed at our earnestness. Finally,

when a man in a business suit, after only one interview,

grasped "the koan of the singing microphone without a voice
    behind it,"

smote his forehead and burst into spacious skies,

we became jealous. *"Here's your own koan,"* the Master
    whispered.

"Don't expect anything of it but itself:

'Why is the Statue of Liberty invisible as the scent of cherry
    blossoms?'"

then smiled his enlightened smile, and bowed off into Satori

or was that the Food Court, at the end of a path of blue tiles.

Cassandra in Connecticut

Some read what's left in tea cups,
Or soothsay cranium bumps, or Tarot cards.
I read leaf shadows on my neighbor's house
As morning sun brooks down among the poplars
Blown by a strong eastern wind. Here's Count Basie
Playing his piano. Here's a buggy ride.
And there's a wolf devouring a man of God.
But where's the kangaroo I saw two days ago
Leaping the Abyss? Where are the three grape clusters?
No matter. Now, in their repose, the shadows form
A Chinese painting of a cliff and waterfall
Gently serene. I climb among dark boulders
Until my neighbor's shape appears behind the screen
Door of his kitchen—and he walks out
Into a forest glade nine thousand miles from here,
Holding his cup of coffee, scratching his side.
                    I envy him
For what he does not see or need to understand
As deer cross his patio, flocks of morning larks
Shadow the face he turns up toward the sun.

April

"Catch me," she says, running faster
> than ever before, long sun-streaked hair
>> floating behind her,
>>> long torso and long legs a blur,

"catch me!" It's April,
> warm from El Niño, with the dogwoods full
>> of blossoms—April in the hills
>>> and April in the valleys. "Hell,"

she shouts, "you can't keep up!" He slows
> just as she'd predicted it would go,
>> this race, this time.... Time flows
>>> backwards as her taunting fingers throw

him kisses when she pulls ahead, her slim
> body leaving him,
>> then vanishing below the highway's rim
>>> he's barely reaching. I'm torn limb to limb,

he thinks—always coming to the meadow last,
> where she's always bending forward from the waist,
>> panting, hands on knees but lifting up a face
>>> half-loving and half-pitying. "Some race,"

she manages. "You know I always win

    but you just keep competing, don't you?" In

        her eyes he sees the April wind

            stream past the boy he was when they began

this yearly challenge... April skies,

    runners' highs,

        the speed and glee of April and the mystery

            of why she's not once faltered so he can slip by.

The Selfishness of the Poetry Reader

Sometimes I think I'm the only man in America
who reads poems
and who walks at night in the suburbs,
calling the moon names.

And I'm certain I'm the single man who owns
a house with bookshelves,
who drives to work without a CD player,
taking the long way, by the ocean breakers.

No one else, in all America,
quotes William Meredith verbatim,
cites Lowell over ham and eggs, and Levertov;
keeps *Antiworlds* and *Ariel* beside his bed.

Sometimes I think no other man alive
is changed by poetry, has fought
as utterly as I have over "Sunday Morning"
and vowed to love those difficult as Pound.

No one else has seen a luna moth
flutter over Iowa, or watched
a woman's hand lift rainbow trout from water,
and snow fall onto Minnesota farms.

This country wide, I'm the only man
who spends his money recklessly on thin
volumes unreviewed, enjoys
the long appraising look of check-out girls.

How could another in America know why
the laundry from a window laughs,
and how plums taste, and what an auto wreck
feels like—and craft?

I think that I'm the only man who speaks
of fur and limestone in one clotted breath;
for whom Anne Sexton plunged in Grimm; who can't
stop quoting haikus at some weekend guest.

The only man, in all America, who feeds
on something darker than his politics,
who writes in margins and who earmarks pages—
in all America, I am the only man.

The Devotion of Thomas Merton

Without density, what is a poem, what is a life
but wind through the trees? Without snarls,
without a crowded race-car track,
thick rich bread or thick rich soup,
how will we be nourished as we work our way
out of ourselves? I've walked light paths,
I've lived in a bare cold room and wept
over a feather. When friends called my name,
I answered with silence. I forgot
books and paintings, history and stars
as single-mindedly, with great devotion,
I focused on a simple piece of thread
and one flower petal. But too soon,
I floated into God before God wanted me,
and became an illusion. No, it's density,
shadows, weight, name tags, tangled forests,
complicated maps of city streets
a poem must wander. Trains hurl
out of the darkness, disease finds many footholds,
crannies, and the mind's unguarded cells;
politicians football through our years,
wars carve and gut us. How can I
ignore the palaces, fun houses—all such cornucopias
spilling constantly? And yet, say scientists,
a pinpoint strand of DNA contains
all that ever was and is and is to be.

Yes, well.... Except relationships, the individual
relation of my pen against this paper,
the room in which I write, old mothy books,
my bell mobile, the traffic sounds and how
they're backgrounds for cicadas, how cicadas
bring back farms I've walked and these in turn
evoke Frost's poem of the boy who climbed
birches and then rode them down, and there's
a famous painting of a laughing boy. His hands
hold a mandolin. Gypsy music. World War II
death camps, the Enola Gay, the day I drove
a woman to a river, hills of Appalachia
tumbling like Zen—on, and on, and on, and on,
weaving layers, pushing buttons, building scenes
and piling blankets, tunneling in them,
carving, molding, giving, fastening
thought to feeling, feeling to the great
density of how we've made our lives
what they are now. And what is that if not
addition—every second adding to this heap,
this flashing glowing bundle of bright coals
we call ourselves? No, I can't go back
to a single lotus blossom in a silent pool.
I simply can't. Not if I wish to bring
the planet with me when my soul flames out
and I am with God, harvest of God's hands,
the changing echo bouncing back—into
the welcome of the ocean of God's will.

Memo from the Desk of Wallace Stevens:

Send me a postcard from
Chile or Tunis to
Tape on my dresser or
Sail through my office.

Let it be frightfully
Luscious or smashing for
Nightmares or psalm-sings and
Scribbles of pencils.

Find me flamingos and
Cats in the jungles with
Faces like moochers who
Thrust out their fingers.

Mail it from beaches where
Waves look like forestry
Ghosts in their gullies that
Waltz in the shadows.

Florida charms me—its
Keys with their looping toward
Cuba, their coral, their
Fishermen bronzing.

Yet, for my needs, if you're
Touring Morocco and
Chance by a view of a
Harbor or ruin,

Post it to Hartford where
I shall be waiting to
Sweeten the world with my
Blackberry mind.

Vehicle

Something for transport. A device
pushed or pulled or driven,
launched, perhaps. Paddled,
rowed across a river, flown
as out of JFK. Something that holds together
while being used: a train
racing a car across Kansas,
a bicycle, a motorboat, even
the Voyager Spaceship. Also,
the medium through which a thing
finds its way home: a novel,
the tenor of a metaphor,
a play, a role, a piece of music
used to display
whatever's shown off in it. . . . The oil
for mixing paint pigments.
The substance of no therapeutic value
conveying an active medicine: a poet
looking from a casement window,
the priest or rabbi holding a dying hand.

THREE

...there have been nights of no talk and nights full of talk. They are never sure what will occur, whose fraction of past will emerge, or whether touch will be anonymous and silent in their darkness.

The English Patient
Michael Ondaatje

The Familiar

We are all to ready to live with it: the nondescript

House on the barren road, trees of no distinction,

The colorless lake beneath the colorless sky,

So long as it seems to work. It has the

Force of inertia, the pleasures of talk

About weather. In its familiar grip

We can lie about ourselves and not be hurt,

Watch clouds hold level in a crystal ball.

But when it doesn't work, when dust

Blows along the road, the lake kicks up, the trees

Flail like the devil's paintbrush,

We hate it—whispering to each other

How dull we've become, how hideous

Your face, my face, our lutulent desire

To be and see and feel and know and touch

Never too much, lest we want more

Than stabs of love and momentary wounds

Healing so soon we soon forget they were.

          We were

Once strangers with our whole lives fit to tell.

On Roark's Farm

The day too beautiful to waste, the trailing arbutus
just under the snow,
we walked the rickrack cowpath by the old stone fence
—*how long ago?*

Long, long ago. Cardinals and early robins fled
our loud approach.
I think we sang; I think we must have said
—*oh, nothing much.*

The tattered fires that dance throughout our bodies
danced higher then.
We skipped and whistled underneath the trees
—*and kissed and ran.*

We found some yellow coltsfoot in an underweave
of mold and bark;
you made my fingers brush the cloven leaves
—*leapt from the dark.*

In the brief space of a meadow you stretched up
to grab the sun.
You peeled it, halved it, gave me it to sip
—*that moment's gone.*

But I undressed you, then I dressed you in the wind
until you felt
it negligee about you, how it swirled and thinned
—*when you reached out.*

Long, long ago—the day high-lofted kites
watched over us.
They rose up from the valley and their gangling flight
—*was rapturous.*

Letter to One Who May Be Dead or Not

I was woken this morning by a heavy wind
    unusual for summer, blowing the curtains
of the eastern window halfway through the room
    in huge flapping gusts

and lying beneath them, giving up on sleep,
    I thought of Wu Li's handscroll,
"Passing the Summer at the Thatched Hall of the Inkwell"
    and his long-absent friend.

What are you doing now? Do you still study
    mist in the branches and the way a stream
follows the easy patterns of a hill
    as it makes its way downward?

I remember the morning
    you decided everything was perfect
and were away for hours in the meadows
    gathering goldenrod.

And how you shut off radios
    with a snap of your fingers, saying,
everything about the world is now
    and needs no reporting.

How have you spent the years? I know
    money upset you. Does the light
still wash away your fingertips, the rain
    still remind you of monkeys?

As for myself, I'm what you might expect
    from someone who forever had his head
inside a book—a bit aside
    from the world and its bearing,

who, this morning, when he watched
    the curtains billowing, and the sun
leap everywhere that it could get before
    wind died and took it out again,

wished you staying here. Who else, in memory,
    could understand Wu Li, the clear
morning after rain, the quiet studio,
    those brushstrokes moving toward the paper's edge?

I got up finally. I drank
    my coffee on the porch and as I read
the morning paper everything I touched
    seemed held out from your hand.

Urban Pastoral

—for Lori

We're going to set up a new detective agency
in a *film noir* city—some building
with rickety stairs
and a neon sign out front. I want
an old black Underwood, a filing cabinet,
one of those rippled glass doors
through which the clients first appear as shadows.

The advertisements for ourselves will be
two lines in the Classifieds. I'll wear
a hat from the 1930s like my father wore,
you'll have frizzed hair,
adjust your nylons regularly
and bend far over in a low-necked blouse.

I'll be moody. You'll be tart. We'll blow
smoke streams at the ceiling fan.
The phone will be a candlestick that seldom rings,
but when it does, your answer will be long
and mine minimum.
Whatever comes, we'll take it on
in our different ways.

You'll work late. I'll stash
a bottle of Jack Daniel's in my desk,
lower right-hand drawer. Sometimes, we'll share,

but more often I'll get drunk alone
and fall asleep, my feet up on the couch.
Next morning, when you open up, I'll still be there.

Somehow, we'll survive: a missing child,
a husband's car left on an empty bridge,
wives wandering. I'll find myself
searching through the mansions of the rich
one day...the next
in the Father, Son, and Holy Ghost
walk-up tenements,

asking questions of the girl with weepy eyes,
the boy who sneers. For years,
we'll float the business on my old convictions
and your pluck. And who's to say
we won't be happy in obscurity,
and sometimes take the day off just for love?

And who's to say the case we're waiting for
will never come?
And if it does—the bag of stolen jewels
your quick thinking spilled, my knuckles raw,
my left side numb,
city hall gone up in flames,
flashbulbs popping in the corridor,

will we stay the same
or move uptown?...Enough of that. For now

I'll watch you polishing your nails,
you'll listen to me hum,
while on the fire escape, the petals will sail off
the red geranium

one by one. I'll read John Donne to you,
his Marlowe variation, and you'll tweeze
your eyebrows, tap your feet.
The nightclub of the city, like a feral cat
we glimpse and lure but never catch,
will leap beyond our sight
and jazz will merge into the milkman's song.

Sunday

—Race Point Beach, Cape Cod, Massachusetts

Benign, the seal's head bobbed among the waves
and at first we thought it the disembodied head
of a large dead dog, a Labrador retriever
or rottweiler, maybe. It disappeared,
but a few minutes later it was floating again,
less than a stone's throw from shore,
ugly, bobbing, calmly regarding us
as if *What were we? How did we come to be here?*,
the huge black nostrils flaring as it turned
ponderously, absent-mindedly, nothing of its shoulderless trunk
appearing before us. A few strokes out
and I believe I could have reached it if I dared,
despite the broaching tides, this part of the shoreline
rougher and deeper than others. It sank again
and for a long time all we did was stare
at the dark shapes of floating seaweed clumps,
shadows in the wave troughs where the wind
arose and abruptly died.... Until, *there*, just beyond
where the waves crested, in that back and forth
jellylike tipping and sliding seasick motion,
the seal's head once more broke the surface,
higher than us now, looking down upon us now
upon our small towels, who were kneeling, looking up
into the huge brown eyes of what we'd almost worshipped.

A Shadowy Government Agency

In the warehouse above us,
forklifts move huge crates from here to there.
The noisy business of the world goes on,
and no one's the wiser.

But down here,
everyone whispers. Even computers
speak with soft voices,
and if we hold each other's eyes too long

someone reports us. We wear kid gloves
even when dressing.
We tiptoe down the brightest corridors. We knock
before we enter

and step to the side, expecting anything,
wary of all. Sometimes we think of ourselves
as poets
adept at tracing odors of burnt rose. More often

we're simply fact-finders,
eccentrics,
odd ducks with a special knack for crunching numbers,
shy, silent people

who disappear next door to you with only a nod
on a warm summer night. What we love
is making plans, and then
step by step transforming them, disguising them

until what comes about
seems purely accident: that car crash,
that falling plane, that sudden heart attack,
the voice that amplified above the crowd.

These were our doings, I think. And yet
who knows?
None of us are sure exactly what we've caused
and what just happened. In our cubicles,

we dream of crows,
small paths running quietly through woods,
the secrets hidden in a field of Queen Anne's Lace,
someone to write our names on anything but water.

Some Man I Knew

Some man I knew, someone you should know,
stood here last night
under this awning. It was raining hard
and left and right across the street

people ran with papers over their heads,
some cursing, some laughing.
Bending ferns of water splashed up from the tires
of passing cars—this night scene a thing

Dufy could have painted well. The man
cupped his palm around a lighter flame,
sucked a sprig of fire into his cigarette,
and stood there smoking with such perfect calm

I swear he didn't care if he'd go on
or stay eternally. Shops closed.
What had been a stream of taxicabs
trickled down to those

few gypsy ones
you're never sure if you should hail or not,
and one by one the lighted windows in the high hotels
around him all went out,

and yet he stood there still,
when not smoking, humming to himself,
I think—the rain not letting up at all,
but falling like increasing wealth

so often keeps on coming to the rich
who have no need for it but like to watch
it grow and grow
until it's just a game of pitch and catch

and store away. Two hours passed. By now
the street had grown so dark, I wasn't sure
if I could stay awake. And if I nodded off,
would he still be there

who couldn't see me staring warily at him
from my dark room,
and even if he could, would never care
if I was safe or if I'd come to harm,

or even if I was. At last,
he put his hand against the rain
and with quick catlike strokes
splashed water on his face. I sensed then

the anguished look of one who waits and waits
far beyond reason,

the calm he had assumed so long,
for a moment, broken,

in the next, regained. Another cigarette, and finally,
head up and striding slowly toward downtown,
his shoulders never hunched,
into the pouring rain the man I knew walked on.

The Back of God

Is covered with whip marks, cancer cells; its muscles
Ripple when lifting weights. Dragon tattoos
Writhe on both shoulders. It is always turned
Against the righteous and the rich,
The meaty slabs of it cold and hard
As if just come from some gigantic freezer room
Or pulled from a river. The back of God,
Only slightly tapered to its buttocks,
Has no expression but what's read or gouged in it,
Is an awful blank stare, a cliff
Wracked with deep fissures. It's decisive
As a full packing crate, its spine
A series of spikes approaching an overhang
Impossible to traverse. Confounded by it,
Armies rage and die. Lovers beat their hands
Against its stiff flesh. It is the disembodied
Torso wedged between two generations,
The living carcass that you throw yourself upon,
Screaming and crying that it is not just
To treat you this way. In its huge shadow,
You ride the dark streets of your firm belief
That love's not charity and never freely given.

Animus

We plan our days, but our days have other plans;
The mood of one affects the mood of all,
As if the hours formed in caravans

Moving out, always moving out, a caterwaul
Commanding us to live our lives as theirs,
Seconds screaming minutes to nightfall.

We clothe our bodies, pad our earthenwares;
Lifting our hands, we shield our eyes from sun,
Anoint our newest journey with our oldest prayers.

This day, we say, there'll be no jettison;
We'll ford crazed rivers safely, top the hills;
We'll fat the meat around the skeleton.

But west skies darken; the good mind imbeciles;
A careless moment spins the frying pan;
New traces break; the mug of coffee spills.

What started promising becomes pedestrian;
The lead's been taken over by the also-rans.
We plan our days, but our days have other plans.

After a Proverb by William Blake

Every day, through lightning over the trees,
the television fog, through conversations
that never veer from malls and superhighways,
you must pull yourself back. Every day,
retreating across the board, watching right and left,
you must lift your hands to ward off evil,
and lower your eyes. The world's a mud hut,
a ring on the street, a stiff breeze blowing
through open windows of an empty Chevrolet.
Should you try to gather friends around you
and hold your ground with silken flags, with snipers
poised in doorway shadows, signaling one another,
a cardinal's wing becomes a martyr's leaflet,
a pond becomes a mirror; candles will turn
into the neon lights of shattered taverns,
jukebox reflections. Every day of your life,
remember that it's all impossible,
hideous, lovely, a Fayerabend maxim.
Hurt and murder are its sole taboos,
love its one calling. Every day, forgive
the weather of Egypt and the thought of Mars.
Touch her inner wrist so lightly she will shudder,
        court the outré.
A lily's to sip from, a sword is to wither.
Take a deep breath, and now a deeper one.

[Say We Have to Name the World Again]

Say we have to name the world again.
What will we choose?
I'd like to call it *Mystery* or *Castle*
and those who live upon it *Leaves* or *Water Droplets*.

But you, with your more somber tones, would name it
Grave in the Darkness.
You'd call breath *wishing* and you'd call the days
Pebble, Crow, Wind, Clock, Shoe, Mirror, Knitting Needle.

Say a plague takes us, say we lie outstretched
beneath *Nancy* or *Michael*
and the forest is *Wistful Feeling*, and that sound
is the computer, which has learned to feed itself.

Can you feel the majesty of Howard,
how sparrows fly through Nancy, Michael's hair is clouds?
Look down the raven, this is Pebble,
we are wishing rose scents in Old Mystery's arms.

If You Get There Before I Do

Air out the linens, unlatch the shutters on the eastern side,

and maybe find that deck of Bicycle cards

lost near the sofa. Or maybe walk around

and look out the back windows first.

I hear the view's magnificent: old silent pines

leading down to the lakeside, layer upon layer

of magnificent light. Should you be hungry,

I'm sorry but there's no Chinese takeout,

only a General Store. You passed it coming in,

but you probably didn't notice its one weary gas pump

along with all those Esso cans from decades ago.

If you're somewhat confused, think Vermont,

that state where people are folded into the mountains

like berries in batter.... What I'd like when I get there

is a few hundred years to sit around and concentrate

on one thing at a time. I'd start with radiators

and work my way up to Meister Eckhart,

or why do so few people turn their lives around, so many

take small steps into what they never do,

the first weeks, the first lessons,

until they choose something other,

beginning and beginning all their lives,

so never knowing what it's like to risk

last minute failure.... I'd save blue for last. Klein blue,

or the blue of Crater Lake on an early June morning.

That would take decades.... Don't forget

to sway the fence gate back and forth a few times
just for its creaky sound. When you swing in the tire swing
make sure your socks are off. You've forgotten, I expect,
the feeling of feet brushing the tops of sunflowers:
In Vermont, I once met a ski bum on a summer break
who had followed the snows for seven years and planned
on at least seven more. We're here for the joy of it, he said,
to salaam into joy.... I expect you'll find
Bibles scattered everywhere, or Talmuds, or Qur'ans,
as well as little snippets of gospel music, chants,
old Advent calendars with their paper doors still open.
You might pay them some heed. Don't be alarmed
when what's familiar starts fading, as gradually
you lose your bearings,
your body seems to turn opaque and then transparent,
until finally it's invisible—what old age rehearses us for
and vacations in the limbo of the Middle West.
Take it easy, take it slow. When you think I'm on my way,
the long middle passage done,
fill the pantry with cereal, curry, and blue and white boxes of
    macaroni,
place the checkerboard set, or chess if you insist,
out on the flat-topped stump beneath the porch's shadow,
pour some lemonade into the tallest glass you can find in the
    cupboard,
then drum your fingers, practice lifting your eyebrows,
until you tell them all—the skeptics, the bigots, blind neighbors,
those damn-with-faint-praise critics on their hobbyhorses—
that I'm allowed,

and if there's a place for me that love has kept protected,
I'll be coming, I'll be coming too.

Then

What came through the fields was a white horse
galloping toward us:
a white horse with red eyes,
snarls of black flies
swirling about it. What came
through the fields had blood on its mane
and blood on its forelocks—and blood
splattered its loins. We stood
watching it come. We said prayers
that it might swerve. We put our hands to our ears
to block out its whinnying.
We did everything
but run. A coven of sparrows rose
from the grass and settled again. Across
the fields lay the broken swath
of weeds its slashing hooves left
bowed in their wake. No god
to protect us! No road
of words we might take—the white horse
galloping across the fields toward us.

FOUR

Still, there are times I am bewildered by each mile I have traveled, each meal I have eaten, each person I have known, each room in which I have slept. As ordinary as it all appears, there are times when it is beyond my imagination.

"The Third and Final Continent"
Jhumpa Lahiri

The Cove

Something was out there on the lake, just barely
visible in the dark.
I knelt and stared, trying to make it out,
trying to mark

its position relative to mine,
and the picturesque willow, the moon-silvered diving board
on the opposite shore. I listened hard
but heard

no sound from it, although I cupped one ear
as I knelt in the cove,
wondering how far I should take this, if I should seek
someone to row out there with me. Yet it didn't move

or grow darker or lighter. Most shapes,
you know what they are:
a rock-garden serpent, a house in the mist, a man's head,
an evening star,

but not this one. Whatever was out there kept changing
from large to small.
The mass of a wooden coffin surfaced,
then the head of an owl,

a tree limb, a window, a veil—
I couldn't resolve it. I ran one hand through my hair
as I stood up, shrugging. I had just turned fifty
and whatever it was that might be floating there

I didn't want it to be. Too much before
that came unbidden into my life
I'd let take me over. I knelt again and stared again.
Something was out there just beyond the cove.

The Day Before Yesterday

It snowed, or did it rain? I think my parents were alive,
   swimming in Sacandaga Reservoir, the Adirondack Mountains
so around them that they seemed inside a crown
   as they splashed and they giggled. President Kennedy
was lifting John-John in his arms; a Peace Corps volunteer
   saw her first gazelle and a woman balancing a pail
of water on her head. Our son went off to college.
   Someone stupid was killing someone stupid for a stupid reason,
I wrote my first poem, I bought my first computer
   and when the screen went on an avalanche of numbers
jostled the future good. What I did is what you did and only
   the details are different. You unlatched a kitchen cupboard,
reaching into it to lift the sun and moon and stars
   glass from the others. On the Pennsylvania Turnpike
a Volkswagen flipped and slid; we saw a side door open
   into the sky. Time, as we know now, is relative
as the strobe light of friendship, the distances
   between intention and the careful consummated act
which may never come to be the way we have imagined
   clothes falling to the floor, a sparrow in the woodshed,
the rocket's red glare. Sorry. Wasn't that the day
   my brother found his cancer, my mother struggled hard
against the ambulance attendants who were lifting her
   up into Death? Didn't the telephone ring late? Didn't my father
lose the feeling in his hand? How the snow came down!
   Every plan we had went out the windows. Just TV

to soothe us into dreams.... I know I'm reclusive,
    a sleepwalker standing by a hedge at midnight
wondering why everything seems one remove away,
    muted, shadowed, muffled, soft, like having water stay
for hours in your ears; like looking through a veil
    at passing headlights on the street; like saying words
that move so faintly on the scrolls of reputation
    they might as well be wings I'm slowly painting
to make the margins less conspicuous. But here
    and there, I wake. Lemon chicken. Snowdrops. Stunning
phrases of Akhmatova, Dante, Catallus, Crane;
    pictures on six-sided tins of Earl Grey tea,
our gray housecats with their windowsill to windowsill
    endless tour of the house. Then I fall back again
into the dreamworld that is ordinary living,
    my feet and mind move by themselves, I can barely
tell tattered shapes of thought from mended shades of feeling,
    walls from ceilings, chairs from sofas, desks from chairs,
so dreamy life is. You say you are real? You say
    I hurt you? I forgot? I never sent that promised
letter of praise? On the day before yesterday
    fish fell from the sky, our daughter drew a line of blood
halfway down her arm. I lived on tranquilizers, lizards,
    every evening read obituary pages in my search
for notices that someone younger than I wouldn't walk
    the local malls or see the current movies....
You learned to drive. You cooked. You flew to Florida.
    Your mother tossed your father's ashes from the window
of a car in Miami's slums. Listen long enough to anyone

and you'll hear such stories—multitudes of them, and soon
the strange will seem the normal and the normal strange
    as a two-parent family, leisurely hours in bed
reading *The New Yorker*.... We were bound to Ohio,
    we were bound to Idaho, we leaned against a guardrail
above the Grand Canyon. You showed your small naked body
    off to thousands at a crowded nudist beach,
a boy from my college dorm became a name our fingers brushed
    on the Vietnam wall. We went to a poetry reading,
I misinterpreted a friend who meant no harm,
    angels visited a meadow in the dark. They danced
until the sky grew light. The Oklahoma Federal Building
    blew into the stars. Dying, say the women and the men of God,
is only displacement. Mystics say that everything still lives
    in the ash of a moment. What was is always mass
and energy: you're nothing, you are in-between, you're everything,
    cards being shuffled in the infinite dimensions
parallel to ours.... I was a sinner. *Save me.* I was standing
    by a road in upstate New York, expanding my collection
of license plates from all the country's states, but never found
    North and South Dakota. *Save me.* Save the smell
of cranberry bogs, mattresses on fire, straw and ice,
    Indian pudding, apples in the cellar, clover stems,
America's new cars. *Save the whales. Save the children.*
    Save the farmers. Save the unions. Save the feel
of a bellrope lifting you a half-inch from the floor
    and the mattering details, individual as each
moment is to any one of us, no matter what we share
    when the ball goes in the basket or the puck goes in the net,

the crowd comes to its feet and screams "Heil Hitler!"

on a Movietone screen. *Secret or horrible surrenders.*
You were the child with velvet eyes. You were the woman

marching for her rights. I hurried back to my office,
observing, recording, relenting. Silence has a way

of stopping history with a shrug, the white flag raised,
a corner nibbled from a city's skyline.... If you

believe in anything, believe that it is possible
when you look over your shoulder with that twist of head,

skipping yesterday, you find such swirls and knots and eddies
it is incredible we have survived our past,

an open perfume bottle on the mantelpiece, the tug of oars,
to be here wondering about what happened then.

Lost Friends

Where have they gone? Carol, who once exposed
    Her perfect body by the fishing stream,
Arms uplifted, rising on pink tiptoes—
    And then she dove

And disappeared from me. Donald, who read
    Descartes at seventeen and after that
Never took another book to bed
    But wed, instead.

Where have they gone? Where's freckled Sally
    Who wanted, more than anything, a house
With a tire-swing hanging from an apple tree
    So she'd be free

Of her mother's whining and her father's woes—
    Where does she live now? Where's Bob,
The baseball player with the upturned nose,
    Those splendid throws

That pinned the runners to his beck and call.
    Has he found happiness? Does Sharon still
Dream of dancing in a Broadway musical?
    And Bill, where's Bill

Who nightly loved to drive the county roads
    From Round Lake to Elnora,
Turning off the headlights of his father's Ford
    So I'd be scared

Enough to write, he said, of life and death
    With some intensity. We'd stop
At Jo Anne's house. Panting with relief,
    I'd catch my breath

And call her through the windows of the car
    To come and talk with us awhile.
Where's Jo Anne now? Is her long hair
    Still black, her stare

Still challenging? Where's Hank, where's Joe,
    Where's Lindsay, Joyce—and Dave and Gail
Who hugged a snowman in the falling snow?
    Where are they now?

Where have they gone? Is anything the same?
    Doris's fear of water, George's grin
As he explored rock rhythms with his set of drums,
    Weird Stanley's glum

Despair at getting anywhere, Marty's way
    Of carving little crying faces in his desk,

Our Eisenhower politics, our gray
    Fear of Doomsday?

And where am I? At sixty-one, I live
    Only slightly less half-hidden from myself
Than I did then. Some years, I've
    Barely survived;

Others, I've climbed around and shouted in,
    Doing my best to live a praising life.
Do they care or wonder in my lakeside town
    Where I have gone,

Or if I'm still around? Where's Claudette
    Who read my Latin on the schoolhouse stairs?
How we did declensions! The lives that we miswrought!
    Oh, *ubi sunt!*

Being Taught

Once a novelist showed me how a whole life might be caught
in a single brief sentence: *She was a woman*
who never walked in rain. Or, *Imagine a trumpet*
hanging from a willow branch. Creating lives, he said,
is half a game and half such desperate feeling,
it would be a mercy to go deaf and dumb and blind,
sometimes. *When he lit candles,*
he always thought of an Edward Hopper painting,
but which one it was, he could never tell his wife.
"Your life, for instance," he told me,
"how might you sum it up—or would you want to?"
If I lie in bed too long I feel my hands
will never stop shaking. "Japanese poets
do a similar thing with haikus," he said. "In fact
the whole of Japanese art can be explained
by mountain passes, butterflies,
robes left untied,
a swordblade misted with blood." We were walking
through a large Chicago mall
littered with cardboard. I watched a salesman
using only his left hand to tie a shoe, a girl
who swore at a mannequin as though it hated her
and all of her friends. *If I'm honest with myself,*
I'll disappear. He said every year or so
he had to concentrate on colors, blue especially,

the iceblue of an Adirondack lake
when it first freezes over, blue North Dakota ranches,
fishscale blue, the powder blue an evening snowstorm casts
in a car's headlights. But then he'd see someone
and the sentences would come again to him unbidden:
He was a man who loved to row dark waters....
....Without intention, she dressed to be undressed....
All their houses smelled like smoke and beer....
He had a habit of shrugging more than normal,
as if a jacket or a cape upon his shoulders
would never quite settle. We stopped to eat
at one of those cheap steak places where they serve
catsup automatically with fries. Our waitress
hummed to herself and looked like she was biting her lips
even when she wasn't. *Animal, vegetable, mineral,*
which am I? Scissors, paper, rock. I looked around,
and all the faces, all the clothes beneath the faces,
the shapes and gestures of bodies
were turning into one line stories and I couldn't
stop summoning them, it made me dizzy:
all these lives that we were taking unawares,
confetti, heads of bobbing swimmers,
a sentence for each life. *Please, when mine is read,*
make it raw and beautiful at once.
                              After lunch, we parted.
"Work," he said. "My work is a ship that sails away
and I'm on a wooden pier, hobbling, reaching out."
A boy at the bus stop corner glanced at him

vaguely...and I could swear that in this glance was how the boy would see his entire life:

figures on glass surfaces, insubstantial, passing.

Jubilate

How many pale blue skies I've walked beneath,
Wildwoods and towns I've entered! I remember
Beaches and flowers, and children in the elms,
Mysterious sayings from the lips of strangers

That swept me for days from one path to another,
Sun on the wings of high white Piper Cubs,
A church door in Nebraska swung wide open,
The profiled faces in a thousand taxicabs

Skittering New York. Once, in the upper ribs
Of a valley at dawn, a field of Canterbury Bells
Rang for me. Once, along a lonely road in Maine
I heard the splashy turning of a watermill

Over a falls that wasn't there...and all
The books I've nubbed and underlined, the time
I slid down in a field to hear Bob Dylan's twang,
My first walk up the snail-ramped Guggenheim,

The trysts, the trinkets, meadows, baseball games,
Lakes, and river bays. I remember hugs and horns
At the end of World War II, and I remember
Every denim jacket that I've ever worn,

My first McDonald's, and the August afternoon
Nixon resigned. Sometimes, I think we're meant
To live our lives as gatherers of all the sounds
And sights and touches, tastes and scents

We happen on. Before the first brown moths
Come cluttering the window screens, I'll think
Of banjos, climbing ivy, New Orleans,
All the Buds and Michelobs there are to drink,

Freihofer's cakes to eat, rocks to kick, the kinks
And crazinesses I'll work some day out,
Cat Stevens singing with his head up in the sky,
This psalm of praise to turn my life about.

Letter to Ye Feng, His Student Now in Iowa

I remember your paper on the Tao,

How your eyes shone when you got each spelling right.

One late afternoon we talked for hours

Outside your dining hall, about the Korean War.

You wore your red nylon jacket all the time

To startle Americans, I think, although you never said so.

Americans are so possessed by things, you told me.

I asked, "And why do you so love your new computer?"

You were amazed when I showed you my worn copy

Of Mao's *Little Red Book*. You couldn't get over it.

When you got sick, you took a long train ride

Down to New Jersey, and an acupuncturist.

I scoffed, but he cured you. You said, "Look!"

And grinning, jumped up and down on the sidewalk.

One night you gave a party and respectfully

Listened to Bruce Springsteen as if he was classical.

You and your guests sat quietly translating,

Heads bowed, sipping your beers. I found that very funny.

At graduation, you insisted on having pictures:

Old American Professor with a Young Chinese

Student in Robes Beside Long Island Sound.

Now it has been a year. In graduate studies now,

You wear a white lab coat and study physics far away.

Physics are mountains to you. You ski down them.

You love the dawning of numbers, the beautiful flourishes.

Here, in Bridgeport, on our campus of a hundred trees,
Xi Ling, your friend, reminds me to say "Hello."

Poem for Li,
In Her White Bridal Dress

"How many miles to China?"
I ask my friend, the student Ye Feng.

"Ten thousand miles," he answers,
"it is always ten thousand miles."

"But how can I get there?" I ask,
"to be at your wedding feast?"

"Take to the river," he says,
"and then take to the sky."

"Where is your bride, Ye Feng?
Will she be blushing and young?"

"She stands at the doorway," he says,
"bidding her parents goodbye."

"Are there flowers around her, Ye Feng,
and lanterns, and gods of the night?"

"Feel the breeze on the mountain," he says.
"Hear bells in the dusk."

"Student Ye Feng," I ask,
"is China so far, far away?"

"Ten thousand miles," he answers,
"it is always ten thousand miles."

Texas Prison Town

"The only French he ever learned was *à la mode*
and went his whole life thinking it meant ice cream,"
she was saying. This was in a small green and brown diner
on the edge of Texas, on one of those spectacular Texas days
when it seems the wind will blow sweetly across your face
forever and ever. "Yessir," she said, "yessir,
he was some fixins." After a while, as we listened,
the talk at the next table veered accountably
onto Death Row prison meals. Last meals. *"Enchiladas!*
Guacamole, sour cream,
and draft beer so swirl-around-on-your-tongue
your whole body starts grinning." Another chimed in, *"No,*
steak and french fries, salsa on the side,
and for desert a shoot-yr-mama slice of yellow cake
with thick chocolate icing. Glasses of whole white milk,
and one of those little white-with-green-inside mints
as you roll out the door." And here we were thinking
Eggs Benedict, poached salmon, Neapolitans,
a spectacular Port, an ancient Chablis—forgetting
this was the edge of Texas where the warden sets
a twenty dollar limit from one local restaurant,
and allows you a cigarette, maybe.... The last three hundred miles
as we'd driven ourselves from New Orleans, life playing with us
its usual accidental games of random A.M. songs,
rest stops, glimpses of strangers' faces, chance encounters
with a cross on a hill,

gray dogs barking,

city sunshine on an emerald ring,

we'd been talking of adjectives, how adjectives

can dull a noun down into mud, or sometimes

send it crazily spinning, as in *twisty* or *rampant*,

weather-beaten, chaotic, windstruck,

and turn a whole phrase into an advertisement for perfume,

an adventure,

or a dirge beside a river grave. The old cliché

footloose and fancy-free had been stuck in my mind for weeks now,

and *hither and yon*. . . . Our recent neighbors kept moving

because "we don't want this to be our last house," they said,

and every few years, my parents would buy a new car

"so this one won't be the last." Then there were

those caravans of silver Airstreams

we'd passed on the road, and big clumps of them

gathered on fairgrounds like cylinders of oxygen. . . . Philip Wylie

advised his travel-book readers never to return

to any vacation spot where they'd been terribly happy,

because they'd ruin it for good, rubbing off the gold,

dulling the palm trees, muting pavilion music. *Gears. Years.*

Proud Mary . . .

rollin' on the river. The object

is to let yourself loose within reason

and buttercups

and old computer monitors. . . . *"The Last Time I Saw Paris,"*

one woman pronounced. Her girlfriends chimed in: *"Save the*
   last dance for me."

"The Last Tango." "The Last Leaf." "The Last Goodbye."

"I wouldn't love you if you were the last man on earth."
"The Last Hurrah." "The last shall be first."
"Last but not least." "He who laughs last, laughs best"
and on and on they went. We paid our check. Outside
in a corral-like parking lot we'd never see again,
on a warm afternoon we'd never live in again,
being the people we'd never be again,
we watched the cars on the highway moving up toward Dallas
for a minute or two (we'd never know again)
and then joined the others, swinging ourselves into line.

Man of the Cloth

Right now, he thinks, right now a woman in Paris
is looking down upon the Seine and weeping
for her lost lover. She's just read *Madame Bovary* again,
Flaubert on her lips, those lovely syllables
half of church bells, half the dirge of rivers
and now, right now, her sorrow feels so deep
she almost knows God.... Thinking this
is like when one dream crosses through a field
of burdock, shepherd's purse, and meadowgrass
into another, one dream vanishes, the next
opens and a young man's walking Provincetown
on a deadly cold night, icicles like barnacles
under the windows of the closing shops,
and the streets are slipping curves. We are, he says aloud
(the man or the man in the dream, he doesn't know),
all bound to be failures, but what we've failed in,
love, pain, friendship, humor, courage,
whether it leans against a temple in the Andes
or shines on a secretary's bundle of familiar keys,
will be lost as the snow. Right now, right now,
a tree in the Himalayas tosses in the wind,
someone's climbing the steps beside Victoria Falls,
shoulders wet from the spray. A child of China
singsongs *Sesame Street,*
an eleventh cousin's poking at a fire, a daughter of Christ
kneeling and praying that the world be good to her,

and much more than a promise.... He thinks of Phil Levine

and Bernie Strempek walking through Detroit

toward iron furnaces. He thinks of seals' heads

cresting up through foam, another dream, this one

the semicircle of a mountain range

he's going to enter. He can see himself

from a bird's eye, a speck of consciousness

seventy miles in the distance as he travels

over and under and at last far out

until he blends into the landscape like all moving things

stilled in perspective, random, circumstantial

as a bit of rock, a spear of grass, a brief

disturbance on the surface of the Plains—and now

he puts on his collar; he adjusts it carefully

and makes his way past lilacs toward the church.

Although the Temporal Is Beautiful

No one prefers a halfway finished thing,
An apple left half-eaten on the plate,
The lukewarm eddy between love and hate,
A ball thrown lightly, a halfhearted swing.

When everything is neither here nor there,
What can I praise and what can I forgive?
All furniture is merely decorative,
The ballerina never floats on air.

I half-reformed my life. It fell apart.
You can't repair a thing left half-complete.
The half-constructed building down the street
Is not a case of ruin become art.

Houses left half-painted, days that can't decide
If anything but gray is right for us,
In their neglect become contemptuous:
We trusted them, and then they went and lied.

Still even worse are those who chat up fame,
Who love intending, but who work offhand.
They roll in plans like puppies roll in sand,
And when they quit halfway, the world's to blame.

The wars we hate most are the wars half-fought.
Left to themselves, they tanktread in our minds.
We're caught forever on their battlelines:
Korea, Vietnam—we're never getting out.

And so the ballad's grief will never end:
... Half-owre, half-owre to Aberdour. ...
I touched a wavecap with a flashing oar
And then went down before the rising wind.

Poem for My Sixtieth Birthday

From here, everything looks like Mozart's hands,
and barley fields. When I almost died,
gasping for breath in a red and silver ambulance,
I kept thinking the city was rushing over me,
one consequence of lying on your back and breathing oxygen
through a small plastic mask. Some months later,
I found myself buying book after book of paintings,
Georgia O'Keefe, Landscapes of the Nineteenth Century,
China in Art,
and didn't know why.... From here,
just beyond the ghost town of my fifties,
everything looks dizzy, as in one of those dreams
when you keep on walking out of enormous forests
onto beaches at dusk. Off in the distance
people or driftwood branches, you're never sure which,
seem to be waiting for a message
or waving to some of those sailboats running so far upcoast
they could almost be shark fins.... Sometimes, I catch myself
losing track of Time, relaxing to its wash, its sound
of sputtering oars and little snags and catches
from popular music.... *I found my thrill*
on Blueberry Hill.... Oh, how I hate to get up in the morning....
Three coins in a fountain....
But you don't know what it is, do you, Mr. Jones?
Afterwards, when I snap out of it, there's this

computer screen in front of me, and it's flashing

enticements and advertisements, links and nooks and crannies

from all over the world.... Those days in the hospital

during my recovery, I'd walk the corridors

and think of how religious was *Intensive Care,*

the dying man in the room next door to mine

terribly trying to control his daughter's life

right down to her last shopping trip. Elliptical thoughts.

Random feelings.... In a book or painting or a piece of music,

I like to find textures such as I might run my hands across,

a hidden cavern, a little joke

hanging by its tail in a shadowy cave,

some meadows, a crocodile, the footprints

of an old philosopher pursued by elves,

for it's the ramble I love, the nonsensical road

leading to the sensible one, or vice versa. The adventure

of going anywhere at all and not returning

the same person I was.... At sixty,

what's so amazing are the everlasting stairs, the raspberry bushes

and Web pages hidden in the dark,

cold wind on a warm afternoon,

sudden connections with the unexpected,

how much less you care about so much.

    And sometimes I can burrow all the way

from under my grudges.

    And sometimes I spend a whole day fishing for poems

in a little blue creek that runs down from the mountains.

    And sometimes I listen to Mozart,

stopping now and then to excuse myself from between the chairs
and step out onto the balcony
over the city, over the long barley fields.

The Litany of Disparagement

When I leave the lake unseen
And the willows weeping green,
The hills, the field, the ravine,
   Pray for me now and then.

When I envy friends' success,
My own life seems meaningless,
I hunch in my own wilderness,
   Pray for me now and then.

When snow lightly masks my face,
White pines are a blur of lace,
And I only quicken my pace,
   Pray for me now and then.

When I cross friends off my list,
Pretending they don't exist,
Caught in my past's trailing mist,
   Pray for me now and then.

When my children's voices are ice,
They hate my self-sacrifice,
How I turn things over twice,
   Pray for me now and then.

II

I drove, but I didn't turn.
I spoke, but I didn't learn.
I warmed, but I didn't burn.
    Pray for me now and then.

Cards held too close to my chest,
I loved the roads running west,
Old shoes and a leather vest.
    Pray for me now and then.

I never reached my floodmark.
The dog is a distant bark.
The tunnel whirls in the dark.
    Pray for me now and then.

The nurse bends low over me,
With hands and skeleton key,
She opens Death's mystery.
    Pray for me now and then.

Pray, for the willows must shake,
Ripples must die in the lake.
I am the life I forsake.
    Pray for me now and then.

This Far

for my daughter

Here, I leave you. There are tins of water
enough to keep you for a little while,
dried meat and biscuits by the pantry door.
Usually, the mice stay pretty quiet.

The view's not bad. Those are my favorite hills,
covered with pines. On a clear April day
you can see small paths among the boulders,
maybe an eagle if you're looking hard.

Try to remember that the telephone
is only for emergencies—may they be few.
Keep the doorsill swept. You can never tell
who will come riding up from the valley.

These are my books, a motley varied lot,
some too much read, some not much read at all.
If you want, replace them with your own,
or use the shelves for toys and flower vases.

You're going to be on your own—sometimes
for months on end. I've found it helps
to whistle frequently or make out lists
of foods you love and states you've traveled in.

The pump is just outside. The clothesline holds
two weeks of laundry if you're planning things.
Fasten garbage lids on tight. Little devils
come from the woods to forage every night.

I hope you like the sound of mountain streams,
by my count three. But I suspect a fourth
is somewhere out there. Every spring
I think I hear it flowing through the dark.

You might listen for it, too. But now
I've said enough, it's yours. And don't forget
I've left you butter in the blue and silver dish
and stubs and stalks of candles you may light.

THE AUTHOR

Dick Allen has received poetry writing fellowships from the National Endowment for the Arts, the Ingram Merrill Foundation, as well as the Robert Frost Prize for Poetry and The Hart Crane Poetry Prize. His books include *Ode to the Cold War: Poems New and Selected* (Sarabande, 1997), *Flight and Pursuit,*  *Overnight in the Guest House of the Mystic* (Louisiana State University Press), *Regions With No Proper Names* (St. Martin's Press), and *Anon and Various Time Machine Poems* (Dell). His poems have been selected for *The Best American Poetry* volumes of 1991, 1994, 1998, and 1999. They appear in many of America's leading journals, including *Poetry, The Atlantic Monthly, The New Republic, The New Yorker, The Hudson Review, The Sewanee Review, The Massachusetts Review, The American Poetry Review, The Yale Review, The Kenyon Review, Boulevard, The Gettysburg Review,* among others. He recently took early retirement from his position as Charles A. Dana Endowed Chair Professor at the University of Bridgeport.